"Nurita De Sane Love (Moncrieffe) writes with a heart that has been broken and is now restored. Hannah had a desire that she knew could only be fulfilled by God. Don't we all have something that we desire from our heavenly father? Doesn't our heavenly father already know? What would you be willing to give in order to have your heart's desire fulfilled? Every once in a while, you find a writer that can catapult you into purpose simply by putting pen to paper. Nurita De Sane Love (Moncrieffe) writes with a resolve to not just capture the reader's attention by telling a story but rather to teach, to equip and to empower. De Sane Love (Moncrieffe) explains to us that Hannah was destined to show a nation what a mother's love and tenacity can birth when she trusts in God. Her writing is what our generation needs to continue through this new millennia..."

— *Prophetess Tanika Edwards, Elder*
New Life at Cornerstone Church

"In *Hannah's Cry* you will read and be inspired by the life stories of Prophetess Nurita De Sane-Love (Moncrieffe) and that of Hannah from the Bible. You will learn how the author and Hannah both got what they wanted and needed by crying, petitioning, interceding and PUSHing for those things: Praying Until Something Happens. While learning to persist in crying, praying and pushing, you will also learn about the tincture of time, patience and waiting on God and on His promises that fail not. Prophetess Nurita De Sane-Love (Moncrieffe), my instructor at the Prophetic Academy, shares with you and I about her life example of crying through trial and until triumph. I wholeheartedly endorse and recommend this book to you for your edification and strengthening so you too can cry, pray, and push through to receive what you want and need."

— *Dr. John A. Babalola, MD, ThD, Presiding Apostle*
Living Water Kingdom Ministries in Long Island, New York

"... Nurita takes her readers on a spiritually enlightened journey into the world of one woman's barrenness, where her desire to bear a child drove her into prayer. This book brings everyday life situations such as lack, loss and disappointment into focus from a biblical perspective, while teaching the application of biblical concepts. I wholeheartedly endorse *Hannah's Cry* — a most transformational read."

— *Bishop S. A. Moncrieffe, General Overseer*
Cornerstone Global Alliance, Measure of Faith Church

"God responds to the cry of our frustration, pains, disappointments, and hurts. As you read this book, may you be inspired to find the solution for your situation in your cry. Nurita writes from a place that many of us have been in life and she courageously, without apology, shared a personal and poignant account of Hannah's experience. This is indeed a must read for all!"

— *Prophet Delon Aaron*
Author of 'Covet to Prophesy'

"To every woman who was wounded at the words of another woman while trying to endure life's challenges, this is the book for you. Written from a place of victory, this book will help you understand the necessity and purpose of your tears. The author has candidly captured the anguish one experiences while waiting on their prayers to be answered, yet being provoked. Worthy of every library, this book will help you understand your purging season, as a season of refreshing, rededication, and renewal."

— *Dr. Alicia Collins, Author of 'Give Me 15'*
CEO & Founder - everythinglemonade.org

Nurita Moncrieffe

ISBN: 978-0-578-27339-6

Front cover design by Harrison Forde.

Editing & Interior design by Crystal S. Wright.

This book is dedicated to my family who watched me cry many a day, couldn't quite comprehend why, but had the faith to follow me anyway.

To my awesome husband Stuart A. who supports all of my seemingly harebrained ideas and still loves me unconditionally: Babe, you push me to be better. I know for sure you were God sent!

To my new children, William, Kenia and Aj, thank you for trusting me.

To my ever-so-wise son, Michael: God blessed me with you. The fact that God trusted me enough to be your mother is beyond my comprehension, but God allowed me to live a Hannah life and bring forth His miracle for this generation!

Now That's Love!

Contents

Acknowledgments

First and foremost, I want to acknowledge my Lord and Savior Jesus Christ, to whom I am submitted, and whose work I do for His Kingdom and His Glory.

To my New Life at Cornerstone Family, my Measure of Faith Church Family, my birth family, all of my friends, ya'll make me wanna go from better to my very best! To the best administrative team ever: you rock! To Crystal Wright my editor: thank you for all you've done to focus me back on this project the Wright) way... you go girl!

To all the Prophetic Watchmen who have written endorsements and believed in this project: I thank you so much for believing in the God in me. To my Sister Apostle Michelle Mc Clain-Walters who encouraged me to write and kept her promise of support: Sis, I am so grateful to have you in my corner.

Thank you to Prophetess Melanie Gleabes, who first gave me a platform to birth this message. To Prophet Delon Aaron who prayed for me... thank you. To The Archbishop Newel (wink) and Prophet Blake, what a production team! You guys rock.

To Elder Harrison Forde: thank you for the awesome cover.

To my son, Minister Michael who is one of the greatest encouragers there is - Thank you, Michael De Sane!

Sissy Aja, Sissy Yvette, Prophetess Tanika, Sissy Krystal, Sissy Bessie, Prophetess Faye, Bishop Alicia and the newest Sissy Minister Marquita - My girls got me covered always; thank you! I want to acknowledge my husband who didn't mind sacrificing "our" time so that I could finish this project. Babe, I love you so much!

Foreword

I'm excited and honored to write the foreword to this new book, *Hannah's Cry*. Prophetess Nurita De Sane Love (now Moncrieffe) and I have travelled the nations of the earth together preaching, praying and prophesying. She is a powerful senior leader and a dynamic woman, who has learned the art of crying out to the Lord.

Prophetess Nurita carries a spirit of breakthrough. She is a woman who has built a multimillion-dollar business and simultaneously planted a new church in New York. I have watched and marveled at her be persistent in maintaining three important postures for break- through: resistance, relentlessness, and resilience. I believe as you read through the pages of this book you will receive an impartation of these key components from her life.

I believe God is restoring the art of crying out in prayer! Hannah prayed, then she cried out earnestly; she persistently and relentlessly pursued the promise of God in her life, and she would not let go until the Lord blessed her. She stood in the face of torment, mocking, and being misunderstood for the way she prayed. She withstood the temptation to compromise, settle for what she had, and give up on her dream of having a son. Hannah's story is the prophetic archetype for women everywhere to pray and never lose heart until they see a release of the promises of God, until they see the enemy's hand lifted off them, and until they see the spirit of barrenness broken and fruitfulness returned.

Through Hannah's story you will see how it is not only the biological birth of a seed that brings the answers you seek. The answers to our persistent prayers of faith and petition are coming in both natural and spiritual forms. There are many women who were once barren who will birth children, but there is still more to Hannah's story that we can learn from.

If you have labored long in prayer over a dream, a business, or a breakthrough idea, could this too be your Samuel? Could the fulfillment of your dream and primary purpose be what changes everything? This is not the time to be silent. My prayer is that as you read through the pages of this book you will be empowered to use your voice like a trumpet. To make your request known to God regarding His dream for your life.

Modern-day Hannahs carry within them the answers people are crying out for. In Hannah's time the people of Israel were in a spiritual drought and had not heard from God for a long time. Hannah was desperate to bring forth a son. Little did she know, that while she was praying for her own desires to be fulfilled, God was preparing her to birth the man who would start a prophetic movement that would change the world and who would be the connecting force that would bring God's people back into fellowship with Him.

Woman of God, the answer to your prayers is coming. Do not relent. Resist discouragement and distraction and be resilient in the face of setbacks and failure. The season of barrenness you are experiencing is not what it may appear to be on the surface. God will answer and give you the desires of your heart. You will see the fruit of your labor.

I encourage you to use this book to fan the flames of intercession. The message in this book will challenge you to grow and expand in intercession. May the truths shared in this book mobilize you to do great works and mighty exploits.

Apostle Michelle McClain-Walters
Author of 'The Esther Anointing' & 'Legendary Woman'

Introduction

Hey Sissy, I have a rather peculiar question. Do you have a smartphone? In this day and age, I would assume that you do. These smartphones have the ability to download apps. Correct me if I am wrong but I am sure that you don't use many of the applications on your phone.

No judgment here because honestly, that's the case with me too. How many times have you needed to delete unused applications from your smartphone in order to make space for new ones, or simply so your phone will run faster? Personally, I sometimes have to get rid of an app or two simply because it doesn't serve any purpose. You have to clear some apps out because they fill up space like clutter.

And if your phone starts to malfunction, you go to the manufacturers authorized service center for they specialize in having the fix for your phone. For example, I have an iPhone, and once I have any issues with my phone, I have to go straight to the Apple store knowing that they will find a solution.

Nobody services Apple products (iPhone) except Apple. So as an Apple user, I go to the apple store when something happens to my phone. They may tell me that I have to reset the phone. So I have to leave it with them, in their able hands and allow them to reset the phone as only they know how to do. Sissy, I'm going somewhere here don't leave me yet.

Here is where it gets interesting. As the manufacturers reset the phone, something happens to all your contacts and apps. Why does this happen, you may ask? It is because your phone was restored to the manufacturer's original setting.

Now how does any of this this relate to Hannah's story in the bible you may ask?... Hmmmm stick with me for a minute.

I am sure you must have heard about Hannah and her case, because It's one of the stories that are usually taught to kids and shared with adults. In short, she was barren and to make matters worse, her husband had a second wife named Penninah tormented her for it. Hannah's turmoil was due to a situation that God Himself not only allowed, but orchestrated. Can you imagine being tormented for something you have no control over?

For Hannah's life was filled with the overwhelming feeling of "less than" that she was operating day to day, but she was never fulfilled.

She felt defective, just as if she wasn't operating to the manufacturers original design for her life. But this was something God allowed to happen.

In Hannah's desperation ... she began to cry. But her cry moved the manufacturer to reset her life. Have you ever felt so desperate in your situation that all you can do is cry? Sissy we can assume that there was a level of intense desperation and frustration in Hannah so bad that it pushed her beyond sad to absolute torment. Sissy can I ask you to keep an open mind, as I try to introduce you to a new dimension to this popular bible story.

But secondarily Sissy, there is something else you will notice after a phone reset ... your phone begins to work optimally. Your cry will bring you to the Lord and your cry will move God to reset your life! Resetting it back to His original plan for your life and back to the manufacturers original setting.

Like the phone, your life will have no more stalls, no more buffering, no more storage issues or glitches. It will begin to work the way it was designed to work because you've cleared out all the things that didn't belong in there. Your crying is cleansing and resetting! The clutter that was slowing it down, distracting you and filling up space needed for new and relevant things.

Do you know that our cry before the Lord initiates the reset? It does girl! It does! This begins the factory reset and allows God to return us to our optimal operating systems! Journey here with me please, let me show you...

Sissy, let this book about Hannah's cry help you to initiate your factory reset and your intense heartfelt petition to God, let your overwhelming cry to made known. Did you know that there were wailing women in the Bible? Those women were skillful at crying. They understood and taught other women how to cry/cry out before the Lord and get God's attention. *Cry to God*

Do you know that turmoil in your life can trigger a cry that makes God respond? Like a mother knows her baby's cry, God knows yours. Whether it's discomfort, discontentment, disillusion, sickness, disease, or distress, God knows your cry. If you have been a Christian for longer than a week, I know you have encountered situations hardships, needs, persecutions, and the like — that have led you to release a cry to God.

I encourage you as you go through this book to first be mindful that God is taking you somewhere.

You present location is not your final destination. In order to make it to where your Manufacturer desires to take you, you must be willing to let go of some stuff — mindsets, people, habits and so on.

Sissy, I will share scriptures with you throughout this book. I encourage you to take note of the ones that speak to you. Highlight them so you can meditate on them later and receive further revelation.

Finally, read with an open ear for that still, small voice. Anticipate God's instructions, convictions and revelations as you go through this book.

When He highlights little things to you, I pray that you won't ignore them. Get a paper and pen, journal and chronicle your thoughts and feelings as your read. My prayer is just like Hannah, your cry will be heard!

—Nurita Moncrieffe

Chapter 1
WHY THE TEARS HANNAH?

> *He had two wives, one named Hannah and the other named Peninnah. Peninnah had children, but Hannah had none. This man went up from his city each year to worship and sacrifice to the LORD of hosts at Shiloh. Hophni and Phinehas, the two sons of Eli, were priests to the LORD there. When the day came that Elkanah sacrificed, he would give portions [of the sacrificial meat] to Peninnah his wife and all her sons and daughters. But to Hannah he would give a double portion, because he loved Hannah, but the LORD had given her no children. Hannah's rival provoked her bitterly, to irritate and embarrass her, because the LORD had left her childless.*
>
> — *1Samuel 1:2-6 (NKJV)*

Hey Sissy, it's me again. You know Hannah is said to have honoured the Lord and asked for a child of her own, and the Lord granted her request. He blessed Hannah with a son. In case you don't know, Hannah's son was Samuel, and God used Samuel changed the world!

Our story opens with, Hannah, her husband Elkanah, Elkanah's second wife, Penninah and Peninnah's children and their travel to the temple to make atonement for sins. Hannah's is greatly grieved, even though her husband favours her more and gives her more than Peninnah. But Hannah is at unrest because she does not have and children. God Himself shut up her womb and to top it off this Sister Girl Ms. Penninah keeps giving Hannah grief about not having any children of her own.

.Can you imagine living day in and day out with someone that torments you about your short comings and ones you have no control over. Have you ever been ridiculed by anyone in your own family? Have you ever had to live with be persecuted day in and day out? Peninnah was what we would call a bully. This was happening at home and reminds me of my youth. I am the youngest of my mother's children and I growing up

I had eczema really bad. My skin was always itchy and had open sores sometimes. I scratched so badly and there was no medication that helped when I had flair-ups. I felt so subconscious about myself.

In school I was teased mercilessly and at home it was worse! My elder brothers and sister treated me worst than the kids at school did. I was tormented at home and tormented in school. I felt so alone all the time. I tried to overcompensate for feeling less than in a couple of ways. I became the *over*-girl. The over-achiever in school, the over-giver, the over-helper, and the over-attention seeker. So, I can relate to Hannah from the onset. She was being tormented in what should be her place of comfort and peace, by a member of her household.

Oddly enough we can gather from the story that this family had a relationship and a real knowledge of who God was for them, because they travelled to make atonement for sins, yet Hannah was still tormented. I think her husband was oblivious to how badly she was hurting because he asked Hannah why she was sad when he was better to her than 10 sons!

Really Elkanah? Do you think your presence makes her feel better about her childless state? That was like putting salt in her wound, because during those days a barren woman was a reproach. Can you imagine the woman in town gossiping about the barren woman. Elkanah didn't feel the pressure of reproach, because Peninnah had children.

The story lets us know that Penninah ridicules Hannah b.ecause Hannah has no children. Imagine the torture. This gives us some background to Hannah's cry. Sometimes you can be so battered, torn up and ridiculed that your only recourse is to cry out in your pain.

You know during Hannah's day, the idea of a woman not having a child, especially a male child meant she was a reproach in her community, family, and household. So, she not only wanted a child, but so badly needed one. You know that in that day women weren't allowed to own property or to be heirs to their husband's property or money, so if anything happened to Elkanah, Hannah was to have nothing. Her prospects were looking quite dim.

Chapter 2

WHAT'S IN A NAME?

> " Now there was a certain man of Ramathaim Zophim, of the mountains of Ephraim, and his name was Elkanah the son of Jeroham, the son of Elihu, the son of Tohu, the son of Zuph, an Ephraimite.

— 1Samuel 1:2-6 (NKJV)

W e all have a name. Some are family names that are passed down generations or some contractions made up of two names put together, like Mary-Lou, Bobby Lee, or Shelly Ann. Some have a new spelling or while others put a new spin on an old name. But each name is given to an individual to call them out and differentiate who one person is from another.

Just as our own parents name us at birth, so it is in the Bible. Names were given at birth to describe the nature and characteristics of that child and most importantly, their destiny. Knowing what your name means can help to understand yourself. You can always look up the origin of your name on www.etimology.com But for our purposes, let's look at the names of the main characters in this story.

Who was this Elkanah guy anyway?

Elkanah means *God has possessed* or *owned by God*. It also says Elkanah was the "son of Jeroham." Jeroboam means *compassion*. Whenever you see "son of" in the bible, it signifies prominence and prestige of some sort. Wow, let me break this down. The man owned by God, was also a son of compassion.

This means Elkanah belonged to something prominent. He was a prominent man in his country, which made his family pretty important too. He was a direct descendant of the tribe of Ephraim, the tribe whose name means *double-blessed*. Ephraim was the second son of Joseph but was given preference over his older brother, Manasseh. Thus,

Ephraim received the double blessing, which according to custom, would have typically been given to the firstborn.

This is an anomaly in itself because only God can change the family order. Ephraim's brother Manasseh was born first, thus entitled to the double blessing. The family line of Ephraim was doubly blessed. Now that makes the family of Elkanah, a family of double blessing. Hello again somebody!

Let's go deeper. Elkanah married two women. He met and fell in love with Hannah who became his first wife. Hannah means *grace, favor* and *entreating in prayer*.

Imagine that! The man owned by God, who is the son of compassion, born of the line of the double blessing, meets and falls in love with grace and favor who entreats in prayer. Wow!

Elkanah's second wife was Peninnah, which means *jewel* or *pearl*, but it also means *hard*. Alrighty then, the Man, owned by God, who is the son of compassion born of the line of the double blessing meets and falls in love with grace and favor who entreats in prayer and then marries a jewel who is hard Aw man! Look at trouble Sissy, It's all in a name. Sissy, it is all in the name!

Sissy, what is your name?

What you think is barren may just be grace interceding and crying out in prayer to move God's hand and save not only you, but your family, your community, and your nation!

> Please watch what you name your children. Their name will call their destiny!

Chapter 3
FAMILY ATONEMENT

> " *Year after year this man went up from his town to worship and*
> *sacrifice to the Lord Almighty at Shiloh, where Hophni and*
> *Phinehas, the two sons of Eli, were priests of the Lord. Whenever the*
> *day came for Elkanah to sacrifice, he would give portions of the meat*
> *to his wife Peninnah and to all her sons and daughters. But to Hannah*
> *he gave a double portion because he loved her, and the Lord had closed*
> *her womb.*
>
> — *1 Samuel 1:3-5 (NIV)*

sn't this section interesting to read? Elkanah is taking his family up to give sacrifice unto God. But he gave Peninnah and all her sons and daughters, portions. Now, what I find very interesting is Elkanah gave a double portion to his barren wife and not the second wife who had blessed him with heirs? What was so special about Hannah that he had to dote on her like that?

I believe Elkanah was a kinsman-redeemer to Penninah. A Kinsman redeemer is a male family member who marries to preserve the family estate and family blood line. He usually married a widow of a close relative in order to keep the inheritance in a family.

This simply means that when someone in the family died, the redeemer would marry them and end up with a wife and those children as dowry. I wondered why the scripture reads; verse 4 "*And when the time was that Elkanah offered, he gave to Peninnah his wife, and to all her sons and her daughters, portions.*

The verse before says Hannah had no children, so why refer to Peninnah's children and why not call them Elkanah's children?

In my mind it was pretty possible that Peninnah's children were not Elkanah's. But I digress!

It further says in the story that he loved Hannah and gave her "a worthy portion." And it says the Lord had shut up Hannah's womb. So, here it is, the Lord had shut up Hannah's womb. In those days, the womb of a woman was held with esteem, for it symbolized either fruitfulness or barrenness. So, the Lord had shut up the avenue of her being fruitful, which was more or less like a curse in those days.

Here is something you have to get in this story. Sometimes in life we are in a position where we are like Hannah. You are righteous and serving God as best you can, but you appear unfruitful in almost everything. Nothing seems to work, and you could even tag yourself as some failure in life. Well, you need not worry, for the Bible declares in Ecclesiastes 3, there is a time for everything. There's a time for release — a time for the fruitfulness to be released. And God shall not be late. Habakkuk 3 reads;

17: "Though the fig tree does not bud, and there are no grapes on the vines, though the olive crops fail, and the fields produce no food, though there are no sheep in pen and no cattle in the stalls, 18: "Yet I will rejoice in the lord, I will be joyful in God my savior." 19: "The Sovereign LORD is my strength; he makes my feet like the feet of a deer; he enables me to tread on the heights. " Habakkuk 3:17-19 [NIV]

Isn't that worth the wait? The Lord is forever waiting to do the good in us, so we need not worry about the outcome. Let's get back to the crux of the story. So, Elkanah gave Hannah a worthy portion.

Sissy, this is pretty interesting, and it further says her adversary, Peninnah provoked her because the Lord shut up her womb. Peninnah, as we can deduct from the story, was a bully. She was Hannah's adversary.

We all have adversaries in our lives. Your adversary could be in your workplace, church or even at home! Have you ever been in a situation where you tried to do the good thing, but that pesky person came to destroy your happiness at the last moment, tried to cut a nerve, or just tried to bother you? Try as you might, that person always has a way of affecting your mood. So much so that at times/eventually, we begin to feel helpless.

For Hannah, her adversary was relentless. She simply could not be shut up. And to add to her pain, the adversary poked her with frustration on her state of barrenness. If you are a woman who has no child, you might be in Hannah's shoes and ask why God hasn't given you the fruit of the womb. You might even think you did something wrong in the past and barrenness is your punishment. The enemy may have told you God is using this moment as a kind of vicarious suffering for all the sins committed in the past.

Hear me: that is a lie from the pits of hell. God would never torment any woman in that way or any way their sins. Christ came and became sin for us and took it all to the cross! . What God does to us, His children, is to show us how to escape from our troubles, and all troubles have a clear, reliable means of escape. Repentance? Prayer? Your relationship with the Father is the key to your escaped, period!.

Can you guess what that is? It's simply *prayer* —petitioning and asking God for forgiveness and then aligning your will with His will for your life. It is as simple as that, and there are no two ways about it.

Hannah's name, as I shared before. means grace, favor, and mercy. And Peninnah, the hard one, the one who was brutish in her acts, always provoking Hannah anytime she went to the house of the Lord to offer her sacrifices. Sissy Just imagine that Hannah faced what being confronted by this woman.

They lived in the same household, ate at the same table, washed the same dishes and both watch Peninnah's children grow all the while being ridicule whenever she asked God to help her conceive. Its enough to push anyone away.

Sissy, whenever she had to go to worship her God, she appeared before her to remind her of her failure and lack of fruit. Have you ever felt that way? I always feel for Hannah when I read this story. There she was already bearing her soul out before the Lord, seeking forgiveness and each time she went to the temple to get before the presence of God and make her petition known, here is the adversary tormenting her. A key factor her is to remember that the bible never mentions Hannah responding or retaliating after Penninah. She brought her grievances and issues directly to God.

Sissy have you ever experienced pure torment while trying to just get to God? I know I have. Sissy you know what, we have all been Hannah at some point. Perhaps you were unemployed, bullied, unloved, abandoned, abused, single, or even childless, and adversaries would be pointing their fingers at you and calling you names. Some people taking joy in your distress. Some rubbing salt in your wound. I can imagine the hurtful words

"It was your attitude that made him angry."

"I told you; you're not good enough

"No man will marry you."

"You will never be rich"

"You never amount to anything"

"He feels sorry for you"

"Maybe you sinned"

And then you internalize these words and begin to fret. You become desolate, believing what they said about you is true. Eventually even begin to loathe your own self. Sissy I've been there. You must combat that with the what the word of God says about you.

God said in 3John 2: *"Beloved, I wish above all things that thou mayest prosper and be in good health."* This is the will of God for you. God wants you to have all the good things in life and make you comfortable. Read on and see how God perfected His Word in Hannah's life.

God was about to turn her sorrow into joy. I've been in a situation where I was so distraught and thought I was stuck in a situation with no hope or way out, and God just came in time to pick me up from my pit of sorrow and shut up all my enemies. Sissy, some unknowingly and some knowingly provoke us. If you have experienced life enough like me, you'll notice that these naysayers tend to keep quiet when the blessing comes upon you. The quiet days are coming. Sissy just live, hold on to the word of God and just live. Watch me work says the Lord of Hosts! Anyway, most times, haters want to even celebrate your fortune with you. Such is the nature of the Peninnah's in our life. Invite them to the table.

Oh Sissy I digress again, girl I always got a sidebar!

As we read on, one of the encounters with Peninnah grieves Hannah so deeply that she cried out bitterly before the Lord and her cry couldn't be heard by people but was heard by God. God moved immediately! We talk about the type of cry in the chapter before had His servant on hand. Although Eli thought Hannah's was drunk and even accused her of such. God used his man servant to speak to Hannah. God will use whoever He choses at whatever time He chooses! (Thank God for God!)

Hannah refused to go home. She had a mission that day to get what she so desired from the Lord, and nothing in the world could stop her. Sissy you have to be so determined to get what you need from God that nothing and no one will stop you, even if you look foolish or drunk.

Be persistent, persevere and push pass all of your fleshly limits and get to God. You may be tired, but push, you may be lonely, but push, you may at your wits end, but cry out before the Lord! He will hear you, I promise!

And even though Eli's spiritual eyes were growing dim, he was still able to bless. (This is a story for another book). In this case, I'll say Hannah reminds me of Jacob, who struggled with the angel to bless him.

21

24: "So Jacob was left alone, and a man wrestled with him till daybreak." 25: "When the man saw that he could not overpower him, he touched the socket of Jacob's hip so that his hip was wrenched as he wrestled with the man." 26: "The man said, "Let me go, for it is daybreak." But Jacob replied, "I will not let you go unless you bless me." 27: "The man asked him, "What is your name?" Jacob," he answered."   *Genesis 32: 24-32*

In Hannah's case, she's crying to the Lord bitterly asking that the Lord bless her like He did for other women. And with her cry to the Lord, the Lord responded swiftly. God answers us always. He is our loving Father, who sees our fault and loves us anyway in us, as such corrects us when we have done a wrong against him.

Here's an example, as parent, we all have children that we would give our world and even a limb for, if it comes to it. That's what we call a loving parent. We have also had times when our children may have fallen accidentally and scraped their knees on the floor, and we hear them cry. In that instant, what would be your response as a parent who loves your child? Let me answer for you.

You would immediately go into protection mode and move swiftly to check out the problem. You do not want to know whether the child was the cause of the injury or not; all you want to know is that your child is safe.

If we in the carnal world can be this loving to our children, talk more of the God who created the universe. Do you think He is too small to solve your issues? God is not incapacitated when it comes to your situation; in fact, he is well able. God is the maker of it all, God isn't too small to solve all our problems, no matter what it is. All it requires from you is your cry, as your petition of faith — just as Hannah learned.

While we are chatting about family atonement, let's talk a little about Eli. I've often wondered when reading this chapter, why was Eli, the priest, outside the temple? In Judaic tradition, no priest was ever seen outside the temple. They were always inside to make offerings to the Lord.

But Eli was outside.

Why? Why was he off his post? God used that too! Well Sissy we can discuss that another day, because we are not talking about Eli, the priest; we are talking about Hannah's unrelenting faith in this book.

(Nugget: leader people know when you are slacking sir/ma'am, It ain't hidden)

Chapter 4

HANNAH'S PETITION, TORMENT & VOWS

> *Now Hannah spoke in her heart; only her lips moved, but her voice was not heard. Therefore Eli thought she was drunk. So Eli said to her, "How long will you be drunk? Put your wine away from you!" But Hannah answered and said, "No, my lord, I am a woman of sorrowful spirit. I have drunk neither wine nor intoxicating drink, but have poured out my soul before the LORD.*
>
> — *1Samuel 1:13-15 (NKJV)*

In spite of her pain, Hannah still had true faith. This was a faith that couldn't be moved in any way.

Eli accused Hannah of being drunk. Hannah was shocked. She couldn't believe the priest held her in such light, so she had to defend herself. "No, I'm not drunk I'm, bitter in my soul! I have no son and this woman keeps tormenting me! I can't eat, I can't sleep, and I don't even want to go home... I'm crying out to God!" No, she wasn't drunk. She further told him she was a deeply troubled woman. She further defended that she has not been drinking wine or beer of any sort. Sissy, not only was she tormented at home but now ridiculed in the streets! My God imagine people bring false accusations against you while you are trying to seek/pursue God —— distractions that make you cry out even louder and stronger!

Sissy, Hannah was simply pouring out her soul to the Lord. And that's a beautiful thing. I had made this statement in italics because it struck me to the core when I read it. She poured out her being, her very being, to the Lord. She didn't leave anything out. I imagine that Hannah's thoughts sounded something like this:

"Today, I'm going to settle it all, if you don't do it for me today Lord all hope is lost. I come to you year after year knowing that you are the only one that can make this happen for me. Please don't forsake me, Lord! I am making my petition known to you today, I am in deep sorrow. I hurt so much! I am coming to the only one who can fix this! Lord, give me a son! Please!"

Who knows, perhaps Penninah felt she was the special one, and that God loved her more and at the same time torn as she may have

even felt bitter that Hannah had Elkanah's love, though she (Peninnah) bore all the children.

So, God, in his most generous manner, responded through the priest, Eli. He said, "Go in peace, and may the God of Israel grant you what you have asked of him."

4. God will always reassure us (maybe through unlikely vessels like this one had just hurled accusations) but we can rest assured that He hears us. Take heed, the God of all peace, comfort hears our cries.

Sissy, you know some people would expect the Lord to come down and speak directly to her, but God spoke through a priest. A priest whose sons were nothing to write home about. Everyone in the city knew how dirty the sons of Eli were and how they dishonored their Father in so many ways.

But God spoke through Eli nonetheless, and she believed the priest. That is what I call humility to the highest degree. She didn't question him. He was still her priest, and thus his word to her is from the Lord and final.

> Stop dismissing people because of rumors. Discern the spirit for yourself!

Hannah vowed a vowed to the Lord in 1 Samuel 1:10-11 (NIV):

In her deep anguish Hannah prayed to the Lord, weeping bitterly. And she made a vow, saying, "Lord Almighty, if you will only look on your servant's misery and remember me, and not forget your servant but give her a son, then I will give him to the Lord for all the days of his life, and no razor will ever be used on his head."

Ever been so distraught that you begin to make deals with God? I've been there more than once. And Hannah was all too familiar with the process too. Do you know that God will hold you to your vows? It is better to refrain from making one, than make them and break them.

A vow is such a serious matter. Webster's dictionary describes a vow as *a solemn promise, or oath or pledge.* Strong concordance describes a vow as a promise to God, a free-will offering. And God sees a vow as such. A vow is a covenant with God and is contractual. God always keeps His vows to us and He expects the same. Little did Hannah know

27

that her vow to God, her free-will offering, her promise, was the very vehicle God would use to bring deliverance back to the people.

For not many prophets were hearing from God during that time and the Priest in the temple was corrupt, unjust, and unholy. The Prophet that was about to step foot on the scene would come through a barren womb in the covenant of a vow, to bring the Word of the Lord back and ratify the covenant promise of not killing off mankind again. Hello Sissy!

I can relate to all of this because, I was once Hannah. I was a barren woman. I cried the way Hannah did. If you haven't been barren before, you wouldn't know how it feels to watch mothers giving their bosoms to their children or talk about how they had weaned their child and how their child is growing up.

A long time ago, when I was in my small library (which is my bathroom by the way) and writing little notes in my notebook and my attention and focused on what was before me. it was painful not to have a child you can call your own. The medical diagnosis cited a in host of issues, from a missing tube to a blocked tube, to imbalanced hormonal levels, and more. The doctors emphasized my missing tube as the primary issue. They gave me their final analysis and told me to my face that I would not be able to have a child. They were so sure of their report. But deep within me, I knew I could carry my own child. God would bless me.

I was a preacher, a woman of God. How could I dare limit the power of God's way? I pondered this to myself. I remembered the scripture, "There is nothing impossible to the Lord" in Jeremiah 32:27. Even though my heart was aching and my soul in distress, I refused to label my situation as hopeless. *It is possible,* I thought. God could surely make a way where none seemed medically or biologically possible.

I focused on that belief. I didn't care about the Peninnah's around me, who gave me their verdicts and opinions. I was standing on the word of God. In fact, I was standing on the very identity of God. I knew He would do more than I ask.

Soon after I became pregnant to my surprise, I actually didn't know until I was almost 5 months along. God had opened up my womb and soon after Michael was born, I remember vowing, *"God, you gave him unto me, now I give him unto you."* These were Hannah's words. And these were mine also.

I dedicated him to the Lord; yes, I have made my son grow in the things of the Lord in the best way I could. I see my grown son today and I am even more resolute about God's power than I was then. I ask you this: Who is like our God? Like literally, who is like Jehovah? The name Michael means just that, who is like our God? No one!

We all come across the Peninnah's every day. Embrace them, they will help push you into your purpose. So, don't kill the Peninnah's of our world, why not you do this instead. Thank them. We have them all around us. As soon as God plants an idea in your mind or a desire in your heart, Peninnah comes and tells you, "Your dream is too big," or *"It can't work,"* or, *"Do you have the resources for that?"* They verbalize every doubt and potential obstacle to discourage you from pursuing that thing.

Just imagine how poor Hannah must have felt. I just had a thought. Do you suppose Hannah may have been feeling distraught, about her bareness and may have had a suspicion that her husband felt the same way Peninnah did?

We all have been there one way or the other. Where everything seemed hard. But that does not matter. God is surely there to pull us out of the quagmire. He loves us so much. Sissy, you know we question ourselves and our love ones love for us all the time. Its destructive to say the least.

Chapter 5

CLEAN HEART

Hannah's situation is one lesson in life everyone faces in a time in their lives. Perhaps, you might be reading this now, and you have such troubles or struggle in your life, and the people you feel that are meant to protect you, end up scoffing at your predicament. Well, you need not worry, for I assure you one thing. You shall come out victorious — yes, all things are possible with the Lord our God.

When Hannah gave birth to Samuel. He was predestined to be a prophet. So now, we can see the priesthood changing from the priestly to the priestly prophet. You can see such prestige and honor God had given to the family. The act of taking the things of the people and handing it to God had to be stopped. For Hannah had given birth to a son of God who would take all of the sacrifices meant for the Lord, and guard it on the altar — I believe this is pretty deep if you understand it.

So, you need to get this one thing. Never you curse the Peninnah's in your life. Don't curse the hard stuff you see while you pass through the journey called, life. Don't curse or cower away from the hard times. Why don't you pray instead in such situations other than crying? Pray and pray for God to intercede.

The one thing you need to do is purge yourself of any doubts, and shame and allow God to change in your situation. There are protocols that needs to be done by you before God can execute his wonderful works in your life. Get you heart right, Sissy!

As we get back to reverence and respect for God. We will find our faith in Him increasing and the Peninnah's in our lives lead us there.

Sissy, remember when we would ask the Lord to check us?

Oh Lord, I'm before you now. Let me check if all is right with me at the moment." There was a time when the elders would say, if you have no respect for the things of the Lord, you could sit in the church and drop dead. Oh Lord! The elders would further instruct us to check yourself outside and begin to ask for forgiveness of sins. But now the question that pops up in the mind in that period is this. "Could it be that holiness and reverence for God are not always with me?" Well, let's explain this further with Hannah.

Hannah had her reverence for God. Eli saw her outside and when he saw her in the passage it illustrates how Hannah cried before the Lord, and Eli was shocked about how her lips moved and her voice wasn't heard. Eli thought she was full of wine.

But my question is, being a priest of the Lord, how does he know the actions of a drunk lady? He's supposed to be inside the temple, before the altar of the Lord always. Well, Eli said, "*How long will thou be drunk? Put away thine wine from thee.*" Again, I beg the question.

How does Eli know how a person reacts to wine?

Hannah answered and said, "No my Lord, I'm a woman, who is sorrowful in spirit. I've not drunk neither wine nor strong drink, but I poured my soul out before the Lord." And in Hannah's cry of weeping and inner toil she was moving her lips and she poured out her soul before the Lord.

That said, Hannah gave her soul and her heart, her whole self to the Lord. She was probably like, Lord, I'm not taking it to my husband.

I'm not going to beg Peninnah or make her have her way, I'm not taking it to my friends, I'm not taking it to my family, but Lord I'm taking it to the one who matters the most, and that is you, dear Lord.

As we do see now, she pours out before the Lord and she says, "Count not thy handmaiden a daughter of Belial for out of the abundance of my complaint I have spoken unto.

So Eli told her to go in peace for the God of Israel has granted her petition that she had asked Him. She further said, let thy handmaiden find grace in thy sight. So the woman went her way and did eat, and her countenance was sad no more. She knew it was done. There was no need to cry again. No need to listen to Peninnah's ramblings and scoffs.

Now, do you know that after you have an encounter with the Lord your countenance is going to change. Yes, after this encounter with the Lord, and after going through with the pain in having Peninnah remind you of your poor state, you'll surely find that you're going to eat and be merry. Everything would be alright in your world. You do not need to force anything on the outside. You will know the Lord would do the wonderful work he promised in your life, and you will have no doubts in your heart at the very time.

Perhaps, you might be reading this now, and you have such troubles or struggle in your life, and the people you feel are meant to protect your end up scoffing at your predicament. Well, you need not worry, for I assure you one thing. You shall come out victorious—yes, all things are possible with the Lord our God.

When Hannah gave birth to Samuel. He was predestined to be a prophet. So now, we can see the priesthood changing from the priestly to the priestly prophet. You can see such prestige and honor God had given to the family. The act of taking the petition of the people and handing them to God was the job of the priest, but now Hannah would have given birth to a son , a prophet who would take all words of the Lord and bring it to the people. I believe this is pretty deep if you understand it.

I repeat: never curse the Peninnah's in your life. Don't curse the hard stuff you see while you travel through the journey called life. Don't curse or cower away from the hard times. Why don't you pray instead in such situations other than complaining? Pray and pray for God to intervene.

Hannah further said, let thy handmaiden find grace in thy sight. So the woman went her way and did eat, and her countenance was sad no more. She knew it was done. There was no need to cry again. No need to listen to Peninnah's ramblings and scoffs.

Now, do you know that after you have an encounter with the Lord, your countenance is going to change? Yes, after this encounter with the Lord, and after going through with the pain in having Peninnah remind you of your poor state, you'll surely find that you're going to eat and be merry. Everything would be alright in your world. You do not need to force anything on the outside. You will know the Lord would do the wonderful work he promised in your life, and you will have no doubts in your heart at the very time.

Chapter 6

TEARS THAT YIELD RESULTS

'd like to tell you about tears and crying. While I was typing this, I was going through Lamentations. Here is one chapter I would like to share.

Lamentations 3 (NIV):

1: I am the man who has seen affliction by
the rod of the Lord's wrath.
2: He has driven me away and made me walk
in darkness rather than light;
3: Indeed, he has turned his hand against me again
and again, all day long.
4: He has made my skin and my flesh grow old
and has broken my bones.
5: He has besieged me and surrounded me
with bitterness and hardship
6: He has made me dwell in darkness like those long dead.
7: He has walled me in so I cannot escape;
he has weighed me down with chains.
8: Even when I call out or cry for help, he shuts out my prayer.
9: He has barred my way with blocks of stone;
he has made my paths crooked.
10: Like a bear lying in wait, like a lion in hiding,
11: He dragged me from the path and mangled me
and left me without help.
12: He drew his bow and made me the target for his arrows.
13: He pierced my heart with arrows from his quiver.
14: I became the laughingstock of all my people;
they mock me in song all day long.
15: He has filled me with bitter herbs and given me the gall to drink.

16: He has broken my teeth with gravel;
he has trampled me in the dust.
17: I have been deprived of peace;
I have forgotten what prosperity is.
18: So I say, "My splendor is gone and all that I
had hoped from the Lord."
19: I remember my affliction and my wandering,
the bitterness and the gall.
20: I well remember them, and my soul is downcast within me.
21: Yet this I call to mind, and therefore I have hope;
22: Because of the Lord's great love,
we are not consumed, for his compassions never fail.
23: They are new every morning;
great is your faithfulness.

Isn't the last verse a breath of fresh air? We all have those sorrowful moments when we feel like the weight of the world is upon us. And what do we do in such moments? Well, we can only cry.

Tears are essential for clear eyesight. They are said to clean and lubricate eyesight. Crying is essential to your life, and it clears your sight. You can stand and begin to cry. It clears both your spiritual sight and your natural sight. Crying helps to clear your vision.

Did you know that when you open up emotionally and begin to cry, that your brain signals the release of 'feel good' chemicals such as oxytocin and endorphins? Those hormones work to minimize pain and improve mood! The Lord created tears to do a whole lot of good stuff — both spiritually and physically.

So, next time when you want to cry, do it. If you are the kind of woman who doesn't want to show her vulnerable moments to the world, then all you need to do is find a corner, Sissy, and pour it all out.

It is crucial that you realize that crying is totally okay. Otherwise, it will be near impossible for you to cry out to the Father the way Hannah did. When was the last time you had a good cry? We all need one every once in a while. I mean that kind of sorrowful moment that leads to snot running from your nose and tears racing down your cheeks.

Why not bring your tissue, lie down on the altar or in your prayer closet, and cry your heart out? Why not cry the way you did when your mom smacked your hand or whooped your butt? Or the way you did when your dad was disappointed in you for doing something wrong?

When you release that type of sorrowful cry, it is said to release something special to God, especially when it's a cry of intercession. Remarkably, crying also eases the tension in your body, which is often caused by anger, fear, grief, and so on. In crying, many things are released.

Let us look at Hannah, for example. She would have felt she was playing around if she didn't cry bitterly to the Lord. And Peninnah had done her part as sent by the Lord, and she had to do what was done to Hannah so that Hannah could forge a way forward.

Peninnah was her point of discretion. Here's a woman that had everything she wanted. Here is a woman that had the kids she waited years for. But this woman came by it so easily. I believe Hannah would have asked questioned God in her alone time. *Why am I different? Am I cursed? Are you punishing me, Lord?* So many questions must have flooded her mind.

Chapter 7

MY CONFESSION

S o, every time she saw Peninnah, she envied her fruitfulness. This happens a lot with our church folks these days and most times in the world. For example, when church people or leaders get promoted, it becomes a season of celebration for this one or the season for that one. The pastor begins to promote the celebrants. But for some envious church folks, instead of celebrating such people, they huff at them or sometimes look angrily at them.

What is in their minds at that very hour is, "Well, I've been serving all this time," and they begin to give the side-eye. They put on an envious show that sometimes you become wowed when you look at them. Just imagine, this is what Hannah went through every day in the hands of Peninnah.

When Hannah went before God, there had to be cleaning and clearing out. But in the middle of such tears, you will definitely go through something subtle, just the same way Hannah did.

We all have experienced such situations when we are trying so hard to repent from something. You say to yourself, "I'll never do such again." But end up doing the same thing we promised never to do and find yourself falling back to what you promised not to do. Then in such moments, we cry and cry like Hannah did, begging God to help us in such times of despair.

Let me share something with you. I was preaching a message, and I said, "Lord, while looking at everything in my life in order, my son doing what his meant to do, my business going pretty well, and my ministry is flowing quite good, not to forget how I'm empowering women like me at many conferences." I further went on to say, "Now, Lord, you talk about a husband and suitable mate. God, when would this come for me?"

And I heard God within me speak. He had said. "You won't have a husband till you cry for him." And all I did was sit there and contemplate the reply God had given me that moment. It was surreal. God said, 'You are not willing to cry out to him, so you don't have a husband."

I was stunned. And God further spoke, "Because the last one made you cry, and you vowed a vow in your pride that you would never let another guy make you cry again. In vowing such, you had shut something down in you. And until you take back, until you reverse the curse that you placed on yourself. Until you break that vow that you made, which says you'll never cry again for a man, then I can't release the man I want for you to you. My dear daughter, you will have to cry again."

I was shocked. The message that I was getting within my head from our Lord was so much to bear at that time. But I had to do it if I was going to get a man that I'd love to bear his name and be a partner to. I thought hard at that moment and asked myself, "If I refused, what do I get?" and God replied. "Then you have no husband, for you must cry for him to be yours."

God speaking to me from within is no surprise to me, for he said, "My soul yearns for you in the night; in the morning, my spirit longs for you. When your judgments come upon the earth, the people of the world learn righteousness." So, God heard all I said from within because you can't hide your words from God. He is omnipotent and omnipresent— nothing in the world can be hidden from the Lord our God.

I didn't want to be hard like Peninnah, where I mock my predicament, set all kinds of markers, and move to get a man of my own. No, I didn't do that.

I had to serve my God as Hannah and cry bitterly to him till he heard my plea. God had to deal with me, and that was by crying and reversing that silly curse I placed on myself.

To reverse the curse that I had placed on myself, I had to make positive confessions. I had to release the negativity in me. I had to go back and revisit that vow I had made. The vow I made in my tears of sorrow. That silly vow in which I said, "No man will ever make me cry again." It was a vow according to God, for I had painfully sworn in my heart, and God sees the heart. It was a vow, and God had to enforce it. There is a variety of stuff you need to go back and clean up. Yes, a variety of stuff you need to revise. We need to clean up all of the negativity we have in the past.

Sissy, you will become your confession. Your words have more power than you think.

41

Chapter 8

HANNAH'S DECISION

> ❝ And she said, "Let your maidservant find favor in your sight." So the woman went her way and ate, and her face was no longer sad. Then they rose early in the morning and worshiped before the LORD, and returned and came to their house at Ramah. And Elkanah knew Hannah his wife, and the LORD remembered her.

— *1 Samuel 1:18-19 (NKJV)*

Let us read this and see Hannah's next act. They worshipped and gave their offering, and they returned home, then Elkanah *knew* his wife. When the bible talks of *knew*, it means they had physical relations. He knew his wife, and the Bible says the Lord remembered her. In her cry out, as she made an obligation to do what she confessed to doing when she had her child, God at the same time had to make his commitment. The Lord opened her womb.

In life, we all have one hard place we dread so much. But you have to cry out so your "womb" can open. Your natural womb and your spiritual womb. There are some of you trying to birth something new to the world, be it a ministry, or a new business of some kind, or a child. You fight, but you don't want all the troubles that come with it.

You don't want to go hard with it. You don't want it where there are some days that you make money and some days that you don't. You need not fear such hard places or Peninnah moments. They are simply hurdles or blocks placed by our God to teach you one thing, and that's humbling yourself at the moment—they are meant to bring you to your knees.

For me, I know in business, whenever it's a hard place, it brings me to my knees. I bring my colleagues in the church to pray about it, to get something done. And most times, when I do so, it works!

Many of us have to clean up some stuff to get our prayer life back in alignment. So, we can get our desire from our Lord.

It further says, "Therefore it came to pass then the time was come after Hannah conceived, she bares a son and calls his name Samuel; which means, I have asked him for the Lord.

And Elkanah and his house went up to offer to the Lord yearly sacrifices, and to vow to the Lord."

Now Elkanah is going up to offer, and all can see Peninnah and her children, but Hannah didn't go because she was wearing the baby. I can just imagine how Peninnah would have felt at that moment. Who was she going to taunt now? And can you imagine how she would have felt when Hannah said she was going to be with her baby and the go-ahead to do as they wish? I so loved this part of the scripture.

"And Hannah did not go up she said to her husband, I will not go up until the child is weaned, and I will bring him that he may appear before the Lord and abide forever." That's Hannah's decision. She was preparing the child before the Lord.

This was the promise she had made to the Lord, and she was going to fulfill it. So, all of the hardiness from Peninnah was worth the wait and the tears of bitterness on that faithful day.

Some scriptures tell us Hannah gave her child to the Lord when she was done weaning the child, while some tell us it was seven years later. But all of that doesn't matter. What matters to me in this part of the story is what Hannah teaches us all. She had to teach her dear child how to grow in the things of God. She had to teach him how to come before God. She had to teach him how to come before a man of God before she dared keep him in the hands of Eli.

And it is far from the warped view that most church folks have, in which they purport or say Hannah felt this need to keep the child—can you imagine such nonsense? Hannah knew her obligation, and she was not going to break out from such an obligation. You cannot cheat God, and Hannah knew better.

Perhaps, she had learned of the way Eli had trained his sons and did not want her child being scorned by the Lord.

We will follow up on some things with Hannah, but we are majorly going to talk about the cry first of all. And after we do talk about the cry and what the cry really is, we are going to jump into some things that beg discussed.

One of the things we began to discuss at the beginning of this book was Hannah's sore place, her place of neglect and dejection. She was in a place where she was most beaten and torn up. She was tattered. And in that place, Hannah had one vow and made a declaration with God. Right there amid the vow, in her saddest place, her most desolate place. The place where she was spiritually bankrupt and beaten by her adversary. In that very place, she cried out.

We read how she cried out before the Lord and Eli because she was talking to herself, and Eli was puzzled on why her lips moved, but no voice was heard. He had thought she was drunk with wine—well, all of that is interesting to read. But today, we are going to discuss Hannah's cry.

We would have to discuss how she wailed to God and what God had to say about crying and wailing in that regard.

In the Caribbean, we say, "She was wailing, oh my gosh, she's crying. She's wailing so much." We do have an idea on crying and wailing, that is, the mechanism that brings such momentary acts. We know for sure what it is when someone is wailing and crying. It is a cry of grief, a pang of anger, a type of pain, etc., but when someone tends to cry spiritually in the way Hannah did, it's usually deep, and the pang of pain lingers.

Here is a little prayer for you as you continue to read:

Father, I thank you, Oh God, that the word is being released like a river, Father activates, arise and impart the readers in the name of Jesus, amen.

When we cry, we tend to have an emotional upheaval, and that connotes being sorrowful. We are sorrowful when we cry because we lack something that we earnestly need. This is what goes on when we cry and has been developed since we were toddlers. If you have a baby or have experienced being with one, you will notice that they would have to cry when the baby needs something to draw your attention. If the baby is quiet, they have not made their demand. This is the same with God our Father. When we cry, he hears us.

And there is always a time in our lives when something pricks us with guilt and makes us cry bitterly. It could be the loss of a job, the loss of finances, the loss of a loved one. It could be just anything.

We all had had an experience when we had a broken relationship, and our world seemed torn apart, tattered, and ripped. It did feel like something was being ripped out of our chest. For instance, you had a boyfriend or a girlfriend you so loved, but the relationship did not work, and you ended up breaking up. Or worse, you had a relationship in the church or ministry. This person was your prayer partner, and you were sure the person would work with you through the hurdles of life. This was assumed as a person who knew your heartbeat, who knew all of your secrets, who knew your weaknesses.

But when they betrayed you, you began to feel this stuff being ripped out of you, which made you want to cry, and you did cry. I am trying to say here that there is nothing new to the human experience; this stuff has consistently been with us for a long while. We are meant to cry our hearts out to our God, and there is no shame in having teary eyes towards your Father.

God persuades us in scripture to, cry, cry and cry. This he called travailing and crying. I have gone to so many seminars in the past years where I watch these women crying and travailing. And people are like, "Oh, yes, I got it. I know what it is to travail," but yet such kinds of people find no resolve in their life, there is no moving forward. Well, I believe you do not mimic a cry when it concerns the Lord. The Lord knows what's in your heart, so if you are genuine in crying, he listens rather than making a show to the public.

We must gear up ourselves to go through pain a little to become really clear on what it means to cry. We need to be really clear and understand what it means to travail. Let us head to scripture a little to see what God says about this, Jeremiah 9:20, "Now, you women, hear the word of the Lord; open your ears to the words of his mouth. Teach your daughters how to wait, teach one another a lament." That says it all, don't you think?

In this light, I'd like to notify you to take notes; make sure you take copious notes because you will have to refer back to your notes later on. This is done so that you have the solution when any situation comes up, and you will know what to do to quell such immediately.

Don't be like, "I know his scripture so well, so why I jot them down." you never stop learning in life. In fact, everything about life is a gradual learning process. Do you know that God's word can have several meanings and solutions? That is how wonderful it is to humanity, so if you are hell-bent on sticking to the literal sense, then you are on your way to ignorance. You need to get the overall spiritual sense of scripture and not the literal sense.

You need to be a scholar when it concerns the Bible. You need to be someone who remembers what was said in that book, in that conference, in that church, and in all events where the word of God is spoken. Write your notes, make sure you take good notes; they are all very important to some degree.

I keep notes of my leaders, be it Apostle Duncan, Apostle Eckhardt, Prophetess Michelle and now my husband and our Apostle, Dr Diane Curry, and the likes. I make sure my notes are ready for me to relearn when I so wish.

Most times, I try to place myself in a position to speak with the leader and have discussion when ministry is finished. I listen attentively and begin to jot down all the juicy information he wants to share with us. The notes I have, whether from the Bible, books, or lectures, I continue to study them..

Going back to our discussion of scripture, it further says in verse 21: Death has climbed in through our windows and has entered our fortresses; it has removed the children from the streets and the young men from the public squares

22; Say, "This is what the Lord declares: "Dead bodies will lie like dung on the open field, like cut grain behind the reaper, with no one to gather them."

23: This is what the Lord says: "Let not the wise boast of their wisdom or the strong boast of their strength or the rich boast of their riches,

24: but let the one who boasts boast about this; that they have the understanding to know me, that I am the Lord, who exercises kindness, justice, and righteousness on earth, for in these I delight." Declares the Lord.

If you check this out, you will see that God is giving some instruction. He says, "Hear ye the word of the Lord oh ye women, teach your daughters wailing, teach your daughters lamentation." Why would God say that? Why would God say teach your daughters lamentation? Now, I push the question to you, why would God say teach your daughters wailing? Why would God beckon us to cry? This does not make sense to the world, but it makes a lot of sense to the spiritually minded person.

It is not only about yourself and your family. You need to teach your neighbors, teach everyone around you how to cry, how to wail. When it comes to the wailing, when it comes to the crying, there is an intercession that goes on when those teardrops. If you remember, I said Hannah vowed a vow in the cry, and God responded. The Father always responds to a cry. And what a cry does is soften the heart of the one who cares for us and make such a person respond.

God, in His benevolence, was instructing them to teach their daughters how to cry. Begin to teach your neighbors how to cry out. How to lament and how to cry out before the Lord. When you teach them how to cry, that would surely soften the heart of the Father and make Him respond to the clarion call.

The one thing I love about our Father is that he surely gives us the answers. He gives us the instructions to do to get our attention. He tells us to worship, and you might want to ask why? The reason is that worship gets his attention, and he loves that too. And as we have discovered in scripture now, wailing and crying unto him also gets his attention.

We also have a prayer. Prayer also gets his attention. God says, "Pray when you pray I will answer you." He gives us that instruction too. He tells us to look out and pray unto the Father who hears us. When we seek God, we would surely find him—that's a surety, and no one can change that.

God has repeatedly given us many ways in the Bible to gain his attention, and none can we lack. And if you observe, all of the instructions God had given are all simple, but a man with his laws and his concept of what he feels God should be like has made his instructions quite hard to ponder. For instance, a man prays, and if it does not work, or if he feels God has not answered, he calls the method baloney and makes a way to reach out to God by performing rituals and sacrifices to gain the ear of God. I'm trying to say that all methods and instructions God has given can work for just anyone. It all depends on the type that suits your personality.

So, please, follow biblical instructions, and not astrology, numerology, and the likes. The instructions of God are true and never fail.

I'd like to pinpoint that verse again. I enjoy it when I recall it in my memory. He said, "Teach the women how to wail, teach your daughters how to wail, teach your daughters how to cry out, how to lament before God.

When we talk of Hannah, we can see how she cried and wailed before God. Hannah was in a sore place, and she lamented bitterly before God. When it comes to lamentation, you tend to tell God how great he is, and at the same time, you are edifying yourself. You are praising God's worth, and you are also giving out a petition during the period.

And why you are making the petition in that period, God listens to you and acts that very second. During such lamentation and wailing, you need to make your vow like Hannah and tell God what you want. And a cry would surely lead you to avow, and joy afterward.

If you read previously, I told you how dejected I was and naked to my soul. I wanted to know why God refused to find me a man, a man I would call my own. And he's prompt reply was, "You're not willing to cry out for Him, that is why you do not have him." and I was like, "Okay, I'll cry out." and he continued with his reply, telling me, "The last one made you cry, and in your crying place and in your weeping place you cried a vow that no man would ever make you cry again."

The stuff here is, some of us made some vows in some hard places about what we would never do. And what we didn't do right is include God in such vows. We should say, "God, if you do this for me, then I'll do this for you."

We, in our own right, took in our own vow and said what we wished to say and how we wanted to say it without considering the instruction of God.

That said, God never has a wish that I would be a single mom, no! That is not his wish for me. As far I was not happy with it, God is not happy. He wants me to be always happy. I am the apple of God's eye. He wishes the best for me and would never falter in his wish for me. He made me be the missing rib of a man that would adore me, that would cherish my every act. That would never condemn me even if I did wrong. But if you are trying to swear or make a vow of your own volition. Then all I can say is, you are heading for a lost end, for you will be filled with frustration if you ever leave God out of the game.

Some people had silently made a vow when they were hurt or broken. For example, a man was created by his love, and the girl he loved did away with him. Then in the silent moment, where he called God in vain, he said, "I swear to God my father, I would never date any girl again." Look at that, and such people would sit and wonder afterward, why is it hard to find a woman?

I'm trying to pass across is never to use idle words carelessly, especially when it concerns vows. Check out Lamentations, and you will find out how humanity often pricks itself with worry and that moment! Aha! That very moment they add God in unknowingly. The moment the name of Lord is added, the vow has been sealed.

God is emotional. You may say, "What?" yes, he is. God is an emotional entity because he is all love. But God's being doesn't sway or act feebly like we flesh-like beings do. He is only in one direction, and that's love. So, it pricks God's inner being when he sees his son and his daughter cry, feeling helpless. At that moment, he has to act, and he does marvelously if you can wait patiently for it.

You need to also note this, when I'm talking about the vow, I'm not talking about magic. This is not something you say a word on, and it appears immediately. Patience is needed with anything that concerns God.

That said, do it now. Cry and see the miracles that would occur in your life. Why not cry to God for better health, for a good job, for a good status in society, for fame, for the best in anything. And as you do so, make sure you believe that God has answered. The basic point here is that you cannot get to God when you don't believe he exists and has answered you.

So, cry. Make sure you cry till the tears are rolling down your cheek—you know that ugly, menacing cry? Do it, and don't back down. As you do so, and you make your vow before God, that is the spot God heals you, and no one can take it back. That is the spot God gives you anything you want. That is the place where he can do wonders.

He instructed the women to go out and teach everyone how to cry. Now, what was going on in the nation of Israel? At the time, it was said that they were captive to the land they were in. The Assyrians were ruthlessly attacking them. All kinds of stuff were going on, and none faltered. Then God had to intervene. He had told them how they were acting on their own terms, and he wasn't happy with it. He was not going to reply to them till they cried bitterly to him.

As a reminder, do you ever wonder why Israel was in captivity in Egypt for over 400 years? But God did not respond till a certain time. Now, does this mean Israel failed to cry all those whiles? I do not believe it is possible. They were held in slavery, whipped and flogged by the Egyptians to do hard labor, and in all that period, no tears of help? The answer is that cries were going on, and there was also some form of complacency, murmurings, and the likes going on there. This is the reason when Moses wanted to help one of them out, he had to curse Moses—in simple terms, he said to Moses, "what is your business?"

This is almost the same thing in our churches presently. There is more murmuring, complacency, and complaining other than crying. You will hear the congregation say things like, "The pastor didn't do that right," "Who does the Queen think she is coming to us like that?" "What is the prophetess saying? I don't understand her teaching?"

For example, I went to register, and they didn't give me my change. I was hell-bent on getting that money back, and the conference price was above the price said after church. Then you head to the registering point to complain, asking them to give you a refund. How dare you? But this goes on in the house of God every day. These are people who believe they are smart. But what they don't know is you can mock the pastor, but you cannot mock God. The same way you ask for a refund for what you offered God is the same way people would ask for a refund when it concerns anything in your life. Simple terms, respect the only true God, seek him, and you shall find him.

And what they do is complain about the problem or gloat in their issues while the enemy still has them in captivity. So, all of the murmuring and complaining is going on while they are sitting in captivity. We all come to church because we seek ways to pull ourselves out of our captivity. And this is one of the reasons Pastors are always here to help; they are here to pull you out of that captivity, that blockade you found yourself. The pastor is trying to draw you out of that captivity; all types of leaders are trying to draw you out and take you to places, the place God has set for you, his son.

You might say, "Captivity? I don't think I was even captured by anything in the first place." And that is where you get it wrong; we are all captured or in captivity in something. You might have this or that type of issue which pesters you and makes you feel so bad that you can't escape. "Oh my, this is not fair. Why would he do that?"

"Why did she talk to me like that?" "Who does she think she is talking to me like that? Where is he? I need my money now." And all types of thought that have kept us in one place, trapped us, if I must say, and there is no escape till we settle down to cry and invite God to the situation.

So, why did it take a whopping 400 years of this suffering of this guilt, of this condemnation? Why did it take so long? This thing was going on for years upon years. Now, what brought them to that point in crying out? And some remarkable stuff happened simultaneously too. God began to raise up the delivered, one who would save Israel from the mess they had found themselves in.

God saw what his people were going through in the hand of heathen, so he said, "I see my people, I see what's going on with them. I will raise a deliverer among them." and he raised Moses and said to him, "You need to begin your training for what's to come." A lot of horrible stuff was happening in that period. One of the popular stuffs that happened in that period was killing all the firstborn of Egypt— that was the first degree by the Pharaoh, and do you want to know why? The Israelites were speedily surpassing the indigenes of the land, and the Egyptians could not take it. Something had to be done. They tried all of the means to decimate the Israelites population, and when they found out that that wouldn't work. They resorted to killing the firstborn sons of the Israelites—how brutish!

And the Egyptians thought they had succeeded, but no man can think smarter than God. God deviated their attention while they still continued the slaughter. Then he took the deliverer, Moses, and kept him aside as the one who would deliver Israel from their troubles. Moses' mother had kept him on the River Nile. She had no name for him yet, but as soon as the Pharaoh's wife saw him, she picked him up and cleaned him. Then she called him Moses, which means "drawn out of water."

53

Well, we all know the story. If you grew up a Christian, you would surely know the story of Moses drawn out of the water while the enemy of the Israelites continued their slaughter. God was there all through the way that he even had to bring the mother, who served as the maid of her son, to cater for him. He grew up knowing all of the Jewish laws and traditions, and by the time he was a young adult, he was well aware of the evil the Egyptians had done to his people—the people of God.

I love to say that God had squeezed Moses and trained him in the ways of the Lord. There is a squeeze now; there is pressure. He is raising up a deliverer in you now, and that squeeze is on. It needs to be drawn from the liquid love of God right in your heart.

There are many situations that you need that tough squeeze to deliver you from the predicament you have found yourself in. Oh, that squeeze that is everything to ask for. And do not think that squeeze is going to come easy. No, it wouldn't. In that squeeze, there is going to be a heart-wrenching pain. A pain that pours every ounce of energy from you, but you need to allow the squeeze to continue. Let that squeezing continue.

Or we find ourselves in a lone place, and we don't get it. 'Why am I here?" is one of the many questions we tend to ask. But if you trust God and know that "All things work together for good to those who love the Lord and are called according to his purpose."

It says all things, not a few things to consider, not just the things we prefer. Not just the things we so enjoy or that we love to endure. No, it says, all things work together for your good, for my good. This just means when they let you go from that job, and you are already thousands of dollars behind your bills and in this and in that, and you still have more bills to be paid. Ask yourself, how are you going to react in such a situation? How are you going to stand tall? Perhaps, there are these children that you need to feed, and you need to pay up your mortgage, and this and that. Let me tell you how to react in such a moment. When the thought springs up, say to yourself, all things work together for good. All things are working together for my good.

Sissy, Once you make up your mind, stick to your decision even if it makes you cry, your cry will be heard

Chapter 9

GOD MAKES THE WAY

> *Wherefore it came to pass when the time was come about the time Hannah had conceived, that she bare a son, and called his name Samuel, saying, Because I have asked him of the Lord. And the man Elkanah, and all his house, went up to offer unto the LORD the yearly sacrifice, and his vow.*
>
> — *1 Samuel 1:20-21 (KJV)*

I remember I was going through a rough patch in my life. I was deep in my thoughts, trying to make sense of my situation. Then I heard the Lord's voice gently say, *"It was good that you got afflicted. Begin to pray that prayer."* I was surprised at what I had heard, but I began to pray. The words echoed in my head. *It was good that I got afflicted. It was good that I got afflicted…*

Not to forget how I asked God about my marital situation, and God still told me the same thing; it was always good that I got into such affliction. God had told me point blank as he gave me some of his magnificent advice that He didn't ordain that marriage. It was my choice, so I had to *"bear the brunt."*

These were points in my life that I sought to make the decisions of my life myself without including God in the picture. God wasn't angry with me, but an absence of him is destruction. No matter what plans you have put in place. I relied on my decisions, my friends, and even my mother. All of these people failed me. My mom is someone I can very much remember. She'll push to do something, perhaps get married, and when it was over and all, she would be like, *"I didn't like him anyway."*

Well, I am not condemning my mom or anyone. I love my mom dearly. But the lesson taught by her experience is, never rely on any man but God. God is the one person who can never fail you. Whether you make your bed in hell or earth, God is always there.

I so want to tell you the story of my past marital life. It excites me to the core to say it. Well, here is how it goes, and here is how my mom taught me a pretty good lesson.

My ex had a conversation with my mom during the time before our wedding. He talked to my mom, and he said, *"If you were Nurita would you leave me?"* My mom replied, *"Well, if I was Nurita, I would stab you in your sleep."*

That was what my mom said. I kid you not. To say I was shocked and embarrassed would be a gross understatement. All I could wonder was *what would my would-be husband think of my mom?* That she's some kind of gangster?

Looking back, I don't blame her. She was my mom, and she could see all the red flags that I had missed or was ignoring. But I could not stop then. I mean, I was getting married. It was my time to shine! What would my friends think if I were to call off the wedding?

At this point, I had already bought my dress. It was a pearl-beaded gown, with a long and flowy train. I knew I was going to turn many heads that day, and I earnestly wanted to show off. Let's not mention the awesome band and DJ who were already hired. We had a three-piece band on our wrist, and everyone was officially dressed for the ceremony. I had on my light makeup and pretty, flurry eyelashes. Everything was set and trust me — it was picture perfect. *And why shouldn't it be,* I thought. *I am special.*

When it was all over that day, I had to settle down to account for the money spent that day. But was I happy? Nope. It wasn't worth it. My ex-husband and I had both spent about $30,000 on our wedding, but we had a two-dollar marriage.

> We had both spent about $30,000 on our wedding but we had a two-dollar marriage.

Why am I telling you this? I went through hell in that marriage. I went through it all, but God told me He had set it right at that time because it was good for me to be afflicted. I believe he was refining me for the mission ahead. Do you know the process of gold being refined in fire? That is what God was doing to me.

God had to let me repeat those words. *It was good for me to be afflicted.* He had to remind me that it was good I got afflicted because that was the only way He would intervene in my situation. Saying those words over and over was the only way for my perspective to shift, and my heart to be open once again.

And the marriage of affliction ended 17 years ago. I simply laugh about it now when I think about it. For seventeen years God's hand was upon me, guiding me towards His best. All that time and all those tears were intentional. Now I am not prideful — just honored. God spent seventeen years refining me to be the best.

I can see now how God has responded to my every cry. When I cried and said, *God, I need a house*, He responded when he saw my heart. In my torment, I cried out to the Lord for a car, and He responded when He saw my heart. *God, I need a business of my own.* He responded when He saw my heart.

> I can testify that the God you serve is neither blind nor deaf.

So Sissy, since we believe He will hear and respond to your cry, what do you do while you wait? I encourage you to keep yourself while you wait on the Lord. You need to serve while you are waiting. When you are in that tight place, that is the spot where God will respond to your cries.

God works mightily and wishes to work way more than you ask or think. He wishes to blow your mind. I doubt Hannah could have imagined that her son would come to save the nation. Let me share one of my situations with you to get a good grasp of what I mean.

I remember another time in my life when God gave me an instruction concerning an issue I had prayed about. God instructed me, *"If you give me the tools to intercede, I'll intercede for you."* Have you ever been in this situation where you prayed for something, and the minute you were done, you found something related to what you were praying about?

For instance, you prayed, and as soon as you were done, you headed to the library, and oh! There is a book that talks about the situation you were crying about. Or as soon as you were done praying, a friend gives you an idea concerning the matter you were praying about only a few minutes before.

You might want to call it coincidence, but as far as I know, there is no such thing as coincidence in God's dictionary. That is just the construct the world gives to a phenomena that they cannot explain. Now, instead of dismissing that book as some coincidence, why don't you take time to study it intensely to get a grasp of what it says of your situation and practice it?

Don't just browse casually like you would a magazine. Read it and study it. Jot down the contents that resonate with you, and when you find one that truly connects, use it and apply it. By doing these things, you are affirming the presence of God in your situation. God will do more, for you have listened to the nudge of His spirit.

Let us look at the passage highlighted at the start of this chapter. The Bible tells us in 1 Samuel 1:21 (KJV) that Elkanah *"and all his house, went up to offer unto the LORD the yearly sacrifice, and his vow."*

His vow. *His vow?* Yes, his vow. Elkanah made a vow before the Lord? But there is no place in scripture which states that Elkanah made a vow. Most of what we read here is what Hannah had done. She was the one who made the vow. In essence, if the wife made a vow before God, the husband has to honor such a vow. So women who are reading this, please do not take this lightly. Do not make vows without your husband's presence. As you read carefully, her husband had to honor the vow. We all have to have our husbands honor our vow to the Lord for it to take effect.

A wife can say, *"Well, I'm making a vow and a pledge to give 500 bucks."* Then the husband says, *"I don't know why she did that. I don't have 500 dollars to spare."* Perhaps her partner did not realize that she made a vow to give before the Lord. Men, your job is to make sure your partner fulfills their vow — this is pretty deep.

For all who are married and those getting married, you have got to learn this stuff. This just means you are going to have to know your spouse inside and out. You need to know their personality.

A wife needs to know what makes her man happy, who are husband really is. And I'm pretty sure that Elkanah was in full accord with this. This was his son Samuel, who was his seed and was about to be taken from him. Not to forget the ridicule Hannah went through before she got that child. You do remember Peninnah and her kids. They were never referred to as Elkanah's children. And it was said, "Let the Lord establish his word..." here is what the Lord had given and who is the man that should deny what the Lord had given and wants to take back. And her womb was open for more children.

She has given something to the Lord, and the Lord has given back to her, pressed down, running over. It was an exchange of trust. The Lord gave Hannah to test her faith, and she did as she was prompted to do, and the Lord blessed her handsomely. So, Elkanah was a man who understood biblical principles, and he never shied away from it.

The woman brought the child to Eli. We talked about her bringing this son, Samuel, up before Eli as an offering. And she brought another offer. She brought bullocks, flour, oil, and all types of offerings to give thanks to the Lord. She gave double, for she knew the rule and the man she was married to.

Anytime your pastor does stand up to the occasion and instructs you to give double tithes. Don't roll your eyes and be like, *"Not again,"* or cringe at the Word. Resist the urge at that moment to calculate all your debt.

You will be tempted to be an auditor on that spot. But God is instructing you in this minute. He is telling you, *give me double.*

And if He is telling you to give double in service, why do you want to hold it back in the world? Why don't you stand up the second time and give the double?

Sometimes we get doubt to hold the full sway in our minds, and we have this voice that tells us that everyone is coming for our pockets in the church.

We believe that since some prophets and other leaders have come and taken from us to fatten their pockets and buy material items, then we should not give anymore. You can just hear them now, *"I come to listen only to the word of God and nothing else."* Well, God is spirit, and He needs a man to do his work. You do not expect God to appear and spread the ministry to the world, do you?

All the Bible prophets were used one way or the other by God to expand the ministry. And they did this through people. Do you want to talk of Elijah, Samuel, Jesus, David? Every opportunity is always the right time to give more than you think you can.

Don't miss the point here. God can do anything. If He wanted to expand the ministry far and wide till it circles of the earth, He would have called the angels to do that. But He has given you that authority to do the needful. And the more you give in faith, the more the Lord is ready to intervene in your every need.

In addition, God didn't change the mechanisms to access blessings just because someone tried to misuse them. If God's method to bless you is through your giving, why not give to the best of your ability? Note that even during Hannah's season of torment and sorrow, she still gave her offering to the Lord.

No, they don't want to be the fool who would give to God; these are some of the words they have ringing in their heart as they snub the pastor's words when it's given. And what is most annoying, and by the way, I've had this experience. This was an experience where the pastor was the only person who stood up to offer to the Lord. Now, ask yourself, how do these set of people desire God to intervene in their situation when they do not have faith as small as a mustard seed?

When I think about the situation, I think about the vow and exchange that I need and what needs to happen for God's word to circle across the globe. I cannot help but give.

I know some people give when they have a situation in their life that they are trying to resolve. This sister had a very serious situation, and even while she was in service dealing with the situation. The Lord spoke and told her to give a thousand dollars. He had to make sure he had given her that money to make her sacrifice.

She came up and said, let me give these thousand dollars because a breakthrough has got to happen in my family. You have to give when it is time to give. You have Hannah, who gave her only child. She had promised him to God, and she was keeping the end of the bargain. She was not going to cut any corners. She was going to give the Lord, His Son. The Lord's son, the Lord's vessel, and Hannah was very aware of that.

I love what Hannah says in 1 Samuel 1:26-28:

> Oh my lord, as thy soul liveth, my lord, I am the woman that stood by thee here, praying unto the Lord. For this child I prayed; and the Lord hath given me my petition which I asked of him: therefore also I have lent him to the Lord; as long as he liveth, he shall be lent to the Lord.

Hannah's vow was for her offspring to be consecrated and holy. Consecrated, meaning *separated unto God and not to anyone else, and not for any other purpose.* No razor of any kind is going to come upon his head — that was an instruction from the Lord — and he shall touch no dead thing. He is not going to drink any wine or eat anything whatsoever that is deemed unclean. He is going to be pure and clean before the Lord our God.

She had weaned the child that she had cried to God for, and now she was giving him back to God.

This was the offering Hannah gave before the Lord.

Chapter 10
DON'T CRY IN VAIN

> " *The righteous cry out, and the Lord hears them; he delivers them from all their troubles. The Lord is close to the brokenhearted and saves those who are crushed in spirit.*
>
> —*Psalm 34:17 (NIV)*

Sissy, I believe God has been preparing you through this book, to release an effective cry to Him, like Hannah did. But how do we go from here to there? You must first see your cry as an offering.

Making an offering to God is an important business. Offerings have a smell of their own. They can carry a stench so foul that you will want to puke or be a sweet-smelling savor that pleases the Father. Our heart condition and motive when we bring an offering dictate the smell that is released. We should always come before the Lord with clean hearts when we present our offerings to Him. In God's sight, your cry is a sacrificial offering.

I do not know about you, but I simply cannot serve my God a plate of dirt. No way.

There is a cleaning up that must happen during the intercessory process. The acknowledgement of God's presence should always be worship and repentance. This repentance happens through true worship but also through your verbal confession and request for forgiveness.

The more you cry out in prayer to God, the more your heart is cleansed by Him. The more your heart is cleansed by Him, the more things get aligned in your life... crooked paths are made straight. The more you get aligned to His will, the more He will release answers and help to you.

We know Hannah's cry was heard by the Lord, because the answer, her son Samuel, is proof. But what brings us to that point of crying? Sometimes, it takes a little pain. Other times, it takes a whole lot of pain.

Maybe for you it's not pain per se, but disappointment, frustration, embarrassment, grief or a combination. Whatever it is, it's enough to get you to the point where you break down and simply release yourself. You forget what you look like, sound like, and even where you are...and you completely bare your heart to the Father.

But what good does crying do? Why can't I just turn to a human confidante and logically find a solution without the emotional upheaval? I won't lie to you: crying out to God is messy business.

Crying out to God is messy business!

It can ruin your makeup, your outfit, and even your schedule but it also:

---

1. Clears your sight which allows you to have clearer vision
2. Brings you closer to the Father

3. Can get God's attention
4. Opens and prepares your heart for God's comfort and help
5. Enables you to pray from a pure and transparent place
6. Prepares you to get answers and instructions from God
7. Makes you feel the *shalom* (peace) of God

So, you need to get it all right. Don't just cry for the sake of crying. Don't schedule a pity party. Scripture tells me that God collects every one of your tears. What happens after you shed those tears is up to you. Are you listening to the Holy Spirit's instructions? Will you obey them?

Change your mindset. Change how you perceive pains and painful issues. If you have the right mindset, you will begin to see the opportunity embedded in each issue or burden that pushes you to release a cry.

Sissy, don't waste your tears. Let your cry reach the ears and heart of the Father, like Hannah's did. Let your cry bring forth change. May you never cry in vain again.

Look out for HANNAH'S PRAYER....

ABOUT THE AUTHOR

" Nurita Moncrieffe (NÈE De Sane-Love)

Nurita's unfettered relationship with the Lord, began in 2000 after receiving a prophetic word early in ministry. Upon evidential emergence of the prophetic office, Prophetess Nurita was ordained in 2007, proceeded with a subsequent ordination as a church elder in 2010 by Apostle John Eckhardt (Crusader Church, Chicago, Ill) and Apostle James Duncan, Christ Church International (Brooklyn, New York.) Prophetess Nurita was appointed by her then spiritual covering to serve as a Lecturer, Administrator and Dean over the Christ Prophetic Academy International not only in the United States but also Internationally.

Prophetess Nurita assisted with the opening of numerous Prophetic schools across the nation, South American and in the Eastern Caribbean. With a keen Prophetic eye, Prophetess Nurita is true servant leader and a much sought-after prophetic lecturer. Prophetess Nurita is a New York State chaplain with a LACA, (Latin and African American Chaplains Association.)

In March 2017 Prophetess Nurita was commissioned to launch a church (New Life at Cornerstone Church) in the North-West area of the Bronx and in 2019 ordained Pastor of that great and thriving work. This year on August 20, 2022 Nurita was appointed as Bishop Designate and her consecration to that office will be held in December of this year.

In her secular life Prophetess Nurita has served her community as a member of New York City's Community Board Council as executive committee board member for Community Boards 5 and 7 and has served as the chairperson of the cultural affairs committee, as well as a youth committee member and liaison for faith-based initiatives.

Nurita is a businesswoman with 20+ years of experience with nonprofit organizations and a string of private Child Care Centers of her own. Nurita not only holds ministerial licensure but secular licensure as a NY State Certified Teacher with a Bachelor's Degree in psychology and Dual Masters Degrees in Early Childhood and Special Education. Nurita is currently a doctoral candidate.

Prophetess Nurita is married to Bishop Stuart A. Moncrieffe, Presiding Bishop of Cornerstone Global Alliance (Elkton, Maryland) and Measure of Faith Church (Stamford, Connecticut) together they parent 4 adult children.